Deb's secret wish
and other stories

Illustrated by Nina O'Connell

Deb's secret wish   page 2

Pat's magic tricks   page 9

The big green snake   page 17

Nelson

Deb's secret wish

"I have made a wish,"
said Deb the rat.
"But I can't tell you my wish.
If you tell a wish
it will not come true."

"What did you wish?" said Pat the pig.
"Did you wish you lived in
a big house and had
ten buns a day?"
"No, I did not," said Deb.

"What did you wish?" said Ben.
"Did you wish you lived on a hill and chased rabbits every day?"
"No, I did not," said Deb.

"What did you wish?" said Meg.
"Did you wish you lived on the moon and sang to the stars every day?"
"No, I did not," said Deb.

"What did you wish?" said Jip.
"Did you wish you lived in a barn and chased mice every day?"
"No, I did not," said Deb.

"What did you wish?" said Sam.
"Did you wish you lived on a farm and chased hens every day?"
"No, I did not," said Deb.

"What did you wish?"
said the friends.
"I wished you would come and
have tea with me.
Here you are.
My wish has come true."

Pat's magic tricks

Pat the pig found a book
of magic tricks.
"I will give my friends
a surprise," he said.

He put on a tall hat and
he found a magic wand.
He wrote a letter to
all his friends.
"Come to a magic party," it said.

Pat the pig put the hat on a chair.
He looked at his magic book and
waved his magic wand.
"Abra-ca-da-bra," he said and
he picked up the hat.

But there wasn't a rabbit
under the hat.
There was only Deb.
Deb was very cross.
"I was asleep," she said.
"You woke me up."
"Sorry, Deb," said Pat.

"Try again," said Jip.
Pat waved his
magic wand again.
"Abra-ca-da-bra," he said and
he picked up a flower pot.

But there wasn't a flower
in the pot.
There was only an egg.
"That is my egg," said Meg.
"Give it back to me."
"Sorry, Meg," said Pat.

Pat the pig was sad.
He looked at his magic book.
"Turn it round and try again,"
said Sam.
So Pat turned the book round
and he waved his magic wand.

Then the rabbit jumped out
of the hat and the flower grew
in the pot and the wand turned into
a stick of rock.

"It's magic," said all the friends as
they ate the rock.

"Look, it's Pat," they said,
"Pat the magician."

The big green snake

Deb was sitting in the garden.
"It is so hot today," she said.
Then she saw a big green snake.

Deb jumped up and ran
down the hill.
"Jip, Jip," she said.
"Come and see the big green snake.
It is in the garden," said Deb.

Jip and Deb saw Pat.
"Come and see the big green snake," they said.
"Where is it?" said Pat.
"It is up the hill in the garden," said Jip and Deb.

So Deb and Jip and Pat went
up the hill.
"It is very hot," said Pat.
"I am hot," said Jip.
"I am hot too," said Deb.

"Where is the snake?" said Pat.

"Look. There it is," said Deb.

"The snake is under the flowers."

"It is a big snake," said Pat.

"I will bite it," said Jip.

"I will bite the snake too," said Deb.

"Oh, it is not a snake," said Deb.
"No, it is not a snake," said Jip.

"I am not hot now," said Pat.

"No, we are not hot now,"
said Deb and Jip.

And they all jumped up and down
under the water.